Vander Cook Etudes

by H. A. VanderCook

Published for:

→ *CORNET or TRUMPET

(Baritone Treble Clef — E♭ Alto — Mellophone)

*TROMBONE or BARITONE (Bass Clef)

(Transcribed and Edited by Walter C. Welke)

E♭ or BB♭ BASS (Tuba)

* B♭ Cornet, Trumpet, Trombone, and Baritone are playable together.

RUBANK®

HAL•LEONARD®
CORPORATION
7777 W BLUEMOUND RD P O Box 13819 MILWAUKEE WI 53213

VanderCook Etudes for Cornet or Trumpet

Revised Edition

6

7

12

13

14

15

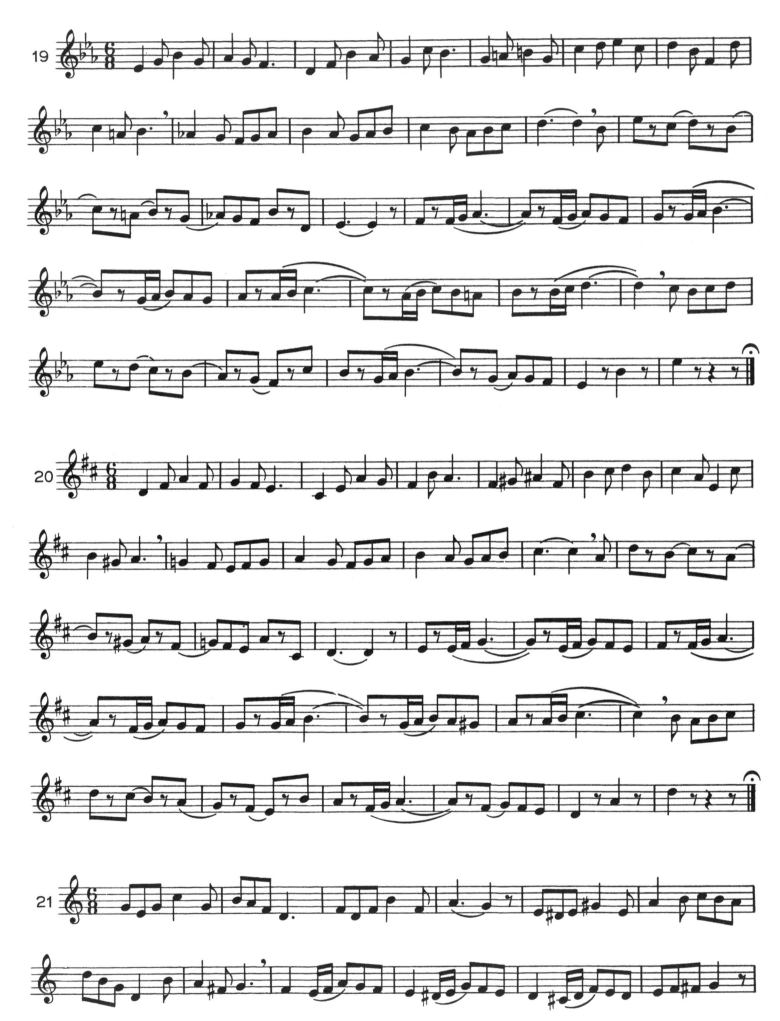

28

29

30

31

32

33

34

Fine

D.C.

35

36

37

39

40

Waltz tempo

47

Waltz tempo

51

52

53

56

57

58

59

60

63 Andante moderato

64 Andante ... faster

slowly ... a tempo

65 Marcia

rit.

66 Andante

67

68

69

Sprightly

70

Grand March

71

Andante moderato

72

Moderato

73

Andantino-delicato

74

broadly   animato agitato

slower

Pesante

Punchinello

VANDER COOK

Copyright MCMXLIII by Rubank, Inc.,Chicago, Ill.
International Copyright Secured

Debonnaire

VANDER COOK

Copyright MCMXLIII by Rubank, Inc., Chicago, Ill.
International Copyright Secured
Copyright Renewed

TRIO

CODA

Vivace

Bonita
Valse Brillante

VANDER COOK

This number available in sheet music form with piano accompaniment.